A TWO-PART INVENTION

ELIZABETH GARRETT

A Two-Part Invention

BLOODAXE BOOKS

ISBN: 1 85224 462 3

First published 1998 by
Bloodaxe Books Ltd,
P.O. Box 1SN,
Newcastle upon Tyne NE99 1SN.

Bloodaxe Books Ltd acknowledges
the financial assistance of Northern Arts.

Cover printing by J. Thomson Colour Printers Ltd, Glasgow.

Printed in Great Britain by
Cromwell Press Ltd, Trowbridge, Wiltshire.

For my children
Alexis and Adèle

Acknowledgements

Acknowledgements are due to the editors of the following publications where some of these poems first appeared: *Aquarius, Atlanta Review* (USA), *Frogmore Papers, Giovane poesia inglese* (Edizione del Leone, 1996), *Making for Planet Alice* (Bloodaxe Books, 1997), *Oxford Magazine, Oxford Poetry* and *Poetry Review*. 'Airlift' was written for *Klaonica: poems for Bosnia* (Bloodaxe Books/*The Independent*, 1993), and 'Love's Parallel' was commissioned jointly by Southern Arts and the Poetry Society for the latter's Poetry Map on the Internet.

I would like to thank Southern Arts Board for their encouragement and support of my work, and in particular for the writer's bursary which assisted in the completion of this collection.

Contents

Cosmos and Mimosa

ENVOI

Go, little huddle of noise, with your A to Z
And forked hazel twig, and ferret out
The man-in-the-street, his multicolour hurt
Furled like a crumpled rainbow. Tell him I said
What I meant when I said: I do. And if he should
Look blank or pretend deaf or say he's heard
That one before, unbutton his doubt to the heart,
To the bloodied fist of hope. Try this instead:

Love, believe; for this is a two-part invention,
Your hand in mine, blindfold, against the gathering
Dark; and it is all we need ever know:
To extricate from the flesh's contrary motion
This perfect interval, Pythagorean,
Irrefutable, and never to let it go.

Vista

Standing, with your back turned, taut at work,
Wearing the day's frosted willow-grey skirt
Like a bell of smoke, while a child went on colouring
Under the spell of the Lakeland-Cumberland arc,
You turned suddenly hearing the doorbell ring.
Turned? No – *spun*, till the skirt flared its carillon
And all the poplar leaves of the world shone
Silver, their green gone in the wind's turning.

And here I am, wise at the open door
Trying to remember what it was I came for,
Struck by a knowledge of beauty years beyond
Anything I had yet come to understand,
Watching you disappear down that corridor
Of brilliant sound, my stolen breath in your hand.

Journeyman

A wheel. A way.
Hub & spokes won't make one.
Rim & flange won't make one.
Stick-in-the-mud-sun –
A golden shaft or a pun
Won't shift it, either way.

A map. A mile.
Cartographers know the trick.
But it only remains a trick.
With a runaway hoop, no stick,
Or the compass's needle stuck –
A contour's a fatuous smile.

A heaven. A hell.
You think that a poem would suffice?
Not even the truth would suffice.
The sun will still rise as if
It were dawn, not Sisyphus,
Heaving his heart up hill.

By All Means Tell the Truth

That nothing could take form from metaphor,
Become, gain currency, appease the roar
Of emptiness with emptiness itself
Is not implausible. Let tongues plead
Innocence of what their speakers seem
To mouth in airy syllables of dream.

Where did it lie: the baited breath, the dream
Half-starved of meaning? Truth itself
Got up in artless beggars' rags would seem
To play the part too well – the audience roar
Approval, swallow it, hook, line and metaphor.
Where, then, the innocence to plead?

Least false the truth unuttered. Plead
The case, then, with the body; and if it seem
Too eloquent a mute – brute metaphor
Incarnate – charge the tongue to quell itself,
Drown out the hammering heart. And lest the dream
Give evidence – silence the blood's roar.

Even the air tells lies: the trapped sea-roar
Of conches, thought-convolved, the ear itself
Believes. Blame words, brand instinct's metaphor
As sham chameleon skin; and if to dream
Is to conceive, then let the sophist plead
His own conceit: condone the right to seem.

Bare facts to naked truth, be what you seem:
Nothing grown rich in a lover's skin. Why dream
Of honesty when one man's lie's the roar
For candour in the face of metaphor?
Whitewash the bone, and still the marrow pleads
For blood's redress. Let sin acquit itself.

Chop-logic in the courtroom. Against itself
The sentence slams its palindrome. Plead
For the guilty, for they are the inheritors of dream,
Of the whoring heart, and the empty roar
Of the word. Absolve the jury of what they seem:
Truth's cipher. I am the metaphor.

'Impossible,' they roar. 'Adjourn the dream.'
As if a metaphor could hope to plead,
'I am the thing itself, not what I seem.'

In Sæcula Sæculorum

In the fullness of fruitfall
We come to this –
Sacked cities, the broken nest,
Our arms aching with harvest.

If to have is to fulfil
Another's loss,
There's equity in the earth's quartered crust,
The pegged body of Christ.

Shores dream of footfall
Through the wash and hiss
Of the sea where each wave is always the first
And hope scatters its crest.

The dry leaves are fretful,
They dispute their lease;
For Spring is a child with what it's been promised,
The world curled in its fist.

Thrushsong... The fitful
Sun disarms us.
What *was* the burden the soul lost
The day it sung its last?

Small Holdings

I

An acre of hope, untilled, a fallow ground
Grazed by the small wind at the back of the mind,
Hearth of heartsease and restharrow.

II

A kernal of grief in the fist, compacted grist,
Locked to the tell-tale tongue in its emptiness,
Seed of disquiet hushed in the palm's burrow.

III

A bindweed of love, untamed, that sings to the twirled
Bud, 'Open, my withywind,' twining the world
And its trust in a ring of bright sorrow.

IV

Harvest of grace, unculled, the cupped hand
Scooped by a thought that blows from the earth's end.
Hollow of loss, or nest, for the lark to borrow.

Gone

And this is the brat
With the brunt of its fist
Bruting the bleak, black keys.
Oh she won't come back
And she can't come back
For I've locked her outside to freeze.

And this is the nest
With the nasty twist
And its eggs like a blank, blue gaze.
Oh she won't come back
And she can't come back
Till the season's mended its ways.

No she can't come back
And she won't come back
Where the frost unstitches the leaves.
And this is the thread
And the undone knot
Of the blackbird's song on the breeze.

Field with One Poppy

For my child's sake I have tried to close
It out, but the light still drenches this room,
Quick at each chink and moth-hole where the rose
Velvet swells and breathes like a living thing.

We are hearth and ember, her weight
Settling as coals do when the fire dies down;
Cheek to my breast, and under this palm
Where the light nests, her pale crown.

Somewhere a child in a darkened room,
Marvelling, made of the torch's trapped beam
A fistful of rubies. How the red streamed
In the fingers' crevices! Like a dream

Of the bulb of the womb, the blood brimmed
With its cardinal mystery, the flame's
Kindling. There is no keeping it out, this light,
Importunate beneath my hand and hooded heart,

And since sleep claims her utterly for its own,
Motherless I will set my daughter down
In the high field, at higher noon
Far from the blood's burden, her mouth

An unfolding bloom, and in her breath
The susurration of the wild grass.

Mortal

Out of the blueblack
Starpocked almanac of night
Staggers a date.
Even the frost protracts
Belief in itself –
Breath on a glass pane –
Heart's halo, fine as a film
Of faith. The hour dilates:
Something that climbs
Into the soul's name
Shrinks in me. I am
Today. A moving, into the light.

Impropriatrix

Fling it out!
Nothing viler than feigned purity:
The mind focusing on white,
The prayer lip-deep. O hypocrite
Disciple of the immaculate –
My promiscuous art!

This is a bastard
Sprung from another's phrase,
But I will love it hard as
If it were mine, fostered
On hope's bitterness
At my own breast.

Unseen and certain,
The gift glides on its own theft
Blameless and inviolate.
The book slams shut
With the midday shock of a shutter
On a square stunned by heat.

Suddenly light shouts –
More dazzling even than when,
High in the bleached Etruscan wall,
That woman flung out
The vast white challenge
Of her sheet.

On First Reading Dante's *Rime Petrose*

Al poco giorno e al gran cerchio d'ombra
Son giunto, lasso

What infidelity was it that stole
The image of the hand that pressed the book's
Heart to the platen, making the blood-black
Ice of that immortal verse distil
Its mortal message here, beyond blame,
Beyond the page's precipice, to trace
The sudden lifeline coursing to the wrist
And take the hidden pulse? In poetry's name
I now lean hopelessly on this – as if
A poem could vindicate the heart's retreat
From constancy; and yet must still forgive
The eye that stole the secret inward of
Your palm, and laid it here, indelible as love
To haunt the midnight margins of this sheet.

The Reprieve

I was a diver then:
In every limb, the coil
And spring of a poem – heaven
Couldn't hold me. Cool
On my flaming cheeks, the air
With its burden of mystery
Cleaved to my passage.
Grace, like a grief assuaged,
A forgiven sin, beckoned
This dark angel to its shadow.
There is nothing the mind reckons
That the heart cannot undo:
See – the miraculous window
Of the water stands unbroken.

Miser

Over the bed's cliff my legs dangle.
It is always the day before dawn
At this hour, wishing myself an angel
Or a pebble — free fall, a way down

Without paying. Against gravity
The heart grapples — irons and hurled anchor
Scouring the air. Nothing will purchase poverty
So well as the clipped coin of hunger.

I shall go out on an empty belly,
Bequeathing to the future my past
And — lest I should sink without trace —
To my memory, love's ballast.

Gift

What riches squandered while it barters
For yet more: this hectoring heart
Hungry for a greed that is its own.
Your gift lies still and suave as bone,
Swathed in its envelope of flesh;
Impossible and real, the veins mesh
And hold you whole. I hear the cool
Note above the rumour of my soul.

That blackbird in the winter rowan –
As in a snood, with berries sown
Myriad and intricate
Into its net – he didn't eat:

But perched, alert and static
On his branch, beholding. And if
He sang, it would be grace unwritten,
Unconditional, no bidden
Quid pro quo, or song for supper –
Which is the most of all the much
We own: by mortal appetite
Leaving the feast untouched.

Unofficial Leave

Distracted for a moment in a grove
Of winter trees all fretted
With the ladder-work of light
And new year's grass unravelling
Its plots – I marvelled
As my soul slipped from its sleeve
Of sombre flesh, on unofficial leave:
Nor did it stop to wave
Or thank me for its stay
But walked right on, erect, the way
A woman's made by love –
Leaving me here to wonder
At my use, abandoned glove.

The Calling

I

It was a day like this when first my unborn breath
Caught in your throat. The sky hung low over Eden,
Pressing you a hair's-breadth closer to earth.
It made the crickets niggardly, and even
The birds grew peevish in their song. You mooched
About till noon, testing my name's vocative
Between your lower lip and teeth. How much
You wanted me then, God only knows: *Eve,*

Eve! – the little sound went, till it drove
Him mad. He rocked you in your body's grave
And wrapped you in a dream to staunch your grief.
So, from the pocket of your breast you pulled
Me, dripping, like a red-silk handkerchief.
Then Eden wept. It washed me till I shone,
Marmoreal and real. That night you wore
The marble of my thigh back to the bone.

II

He freed her from her element to swim
Among the pomegranates and acanthus,
Chiselling the bedrock of her sin
Until she floated. Prone and pensive,
Gislebertus' Eve,
Half reptile, half amphibian,
Wholly human, trails an arm
And does not know it, like a dorsal fin.

This is the flesh steadying; the instinct
In the hand that closes, heedless,
On the fruit's ballast – fearful not of fall
But sinking. She cups her chin,
Her eyes turned inwards on a thing lost
Long before the knowledge of its having.
It moved upon the surface of the deep,
Nor would it heed the cupped hand calling.

Unguentarium

18. Unguentarium: bird. Italian
1st century A.D.

That night, all night, he lay on his back
Sleepless, watching the stars track
Like bubbles in the cool blue glass
That was his passion. By dawn
The bird had come to nest in the palm
Of his mind, almost weightless,
From the nib of its beak to the tail
A seamless sweep of apothecary blue.

And as the gaffers gossiped of the latest –
The loose woman washing with the unguent
Of her tears the strange man's feet –
He gathered into his lungs
All the faith of his marvellous new art,

And dipping the pontil into the molten glass
Blew life – the curve of the breast
Of the bird, swinging it through thin air
Down to the stone cold marver,
Burnishing; then again through fire

Retracing the tilt of the nape of her neck
As she stooped at her heart's business,
His lungs coaxing the pliant glass
And the bird-form blooming – into the vessel
That would bear the soul, the precise
Cast of the glass-blower's breath
Down two thousand years of incalculable loss
Intact, like some miraculous fossil.

Small Grey Bird

Forgetting is the small grey bird
Unclassified, that brags no song,
Begs little lodging, less board –
A traveller in a closed season;
Will nest in the heart's furrow
Unnoticed, feathering sleep
With such luxury of sorrow
That the dreamer, waking, weeps
For sheer joy of letting go.
And though he'll swear to nights
Of unbroken vigil, disown
The imprint in the pillow, deny
All evidence: still he must own
Ignorance of what dispossessed
The heart – its light abandoned nest.

Song

He recalled for her the lost thread
Of her voice gathering the night's length
Into pucker and pleat for a valance.

There was room in the bed for one.
He made space in the crook of his arm,
In the crib of his groin, in the maze

Of his ear, for her father, her mother,
Their lovers, the seasons and years
Of her being. She recalled to him

The dawn, its encroaching grey,
The narrowness of his long home,
Eggs in the wren's nest cooling.

Prints

How deep is it with you? Snowfall,
Footfall, O rich ephemeral handful.
Fleece-lined your palm, your crimson knuckle.

Still the glass falls. Hedgerows,
Bolstered, plump their vast pillows.
Soft it may be – and pure – the snow's

A spartan couch for loving; nor
Would you linger there to read the spoor
Of hare and deer: ours is a morse

Illiterates could cipher. Breathe
On the glass and circumvent the weather,
Snow thaws to the same bare truth.

Love holds us lovingly apart,
Which is a wisdom – and an art.

Winged

I had a page and
The page had words;
Out of my eyes they fled
Like a paradise bird;
Out of the double spread
Of my hands.

In the book's gutter
The mind minds its business
As litter does. What *are*
The letters of love? Close,
Let it close on this
As the wings of a butterfly
On its colours.

It is one more forgetting
To recall me by.

Transposition

It is clear now, in the occlusion of your eyes'
Uncompromising blue, that I recalled
Allas, the Puy d'Issolud, not for the lost
Clapper of that bell that is my tongue
But for Anton, the silent blue-eyed Dutchman;
Who – when my sister knelt in the flame
Of her fifteenth year to drink at the legendary
Well – reined in the dangerous grasses
Of her hair; and how when his fist cinched
That wild sheaf, something in me tensed
Then flexed, watching the ripples' contrapuntal
Spread; and why with the same bleak curiosity
Of my eleven years I trace the course
Of that dark stretto and its aftermath
Back to my mouth, where no reflection is.

Anatomy of Departure

As the two ripe halves
Of a heart, our apportioned selves

Part cleanly at the thrill
Of the ball in the whistle's belly;

Only my child in the crook
Of your arm will not unhook

His gaze – exact, dispassionate –
From where I was, stepping out

Of my skin, my skeleton,
Bone by bone, dismantling.

Imago

When I returned
You had the stillness of the garden
On you. No one called,
You said, but silence –
Though the bees passed through like merchants
With their sacks of gold.

I believed;
And felt that distance spread, then close
Between us, as the hinged
Leaves of butterflies –
Love to love's own blind image
So trustingly inclines.

Hours later,
With a lepidopterist's cool passion
You recalled the one visit:
How, when the Painted Lady
Settled on your heart, her thorax thrilled
With the listening of it.

Alliance française

You wrestle with your tongue
As in a love affair gone wrong –
All gutturals and labials
Confused. My loud-mouthed tulips
Loll and ululate, their lips
Are wide, are red, as any Jezebel.

Words I eat, am utterly
At home in this bazaar of buttered,
Slippery sounds. My tongue
Is where I think; and any
Body's language is a honey
Spiked with salt to ruminate upon.

Darling, must we differ?
How can I watch you shuffle
Genders dumbly and not love
You still? Look, the tulips
Solicit you with parted lips,
Their lingua franca pollen on your sleeve.

Tyranny of Choice

Pick a card, any card
You'll say. I love this trick –
The tease and tyranny of choice –
The dove's tail tender
On your fine and hidden fingers,
And the thumb I'm under.

You know my Queen of Hearts
By the dog-ear on her top-left
Bottom-right corner;
By the voluptuous sad mouth
Which will not smile,
Whichever way you turn her.

Love's Parallel

Since, in the loop of time this will return
To where it began – the poem unwritten
And the heartland squared and folded
On itself – know that last night I followed

A thought of you to the sheer face of love,
My only bearings the imperative of
Displacement, here, in a foreign bed,
Your absent body plotting a curve

Against mine. Something about the cold
Flank of the hill I lay below, curled
Like a fossil, resisted the mind's compass,
Halting here, dark as despair's impasse

Till dawn. Till this – this alchemy of frost
Defining the hill's entire circumference,
So, from the summit, what the map withheld
Of magnitude lies suddenly revealed:

For distance is our love's cool parallel,
And ours the chaste harmony of this hill's
Contours – that neither break, nor touch, but hold
The heart's sheer gradient, encircled.

The Phrygian Mode

They will say we stole it; like the sweet
Music laced with Athene's breath
That Marsyas wooed, even to his death –
A stripped reed, a stopped flute.

Put your mouth to my mouth, but do not kiss:
Say the gods are kind, say they are not jealous.
So, we shall sing when the future flays
Our shadows from us and the hoar frost
Blossoms in the wound. What is Marsyas
And the blood's cry curdling on the breath
But a figure of speech, an old myth?

Put your lips to my lips: it is no fault
Our two souls mingle in the one breath,
Since the gods will judge, and even death
Steals music from the bone's flute.

Paris Matins

Plain song. This one note drawn
Out long and questing like the rope that dawn
Lets mercilessly down while sleepers dream of drowning.

Hoist and winch. A shutter clatters.
Forgive the bleak blackbird its lack of coloratura,
It is as fitting as a glove of water, and the dawn's collateral.

They float like poisoned fish, their bellies
White and vulnerable as sky. A small bell
Mocks the desolate appeal of echoes volleyed wall to wall.

Dies mali. The sun has got the evil
Eye today, dancing the dance of seven veils
Slow motion; something sleek and treacherous unravels

In the minds of businessmen. The Seine
Rolls over in her sleep, where Notre Dame stands sentinel
Above the sheets that ripple platinum and eau de nil.

At the Île St Louis she opened
Her thighs and again at the Île de la Cité. What happened
Then is history. Each heard his own dream break in full diapason

And swore never again to despair
When hauled from drowning. Slowly the crowds dispersed.
Some say – though words are not empirical – her breasts
were like the apples of Hesperides.

Ribes rubrum

Light's rosary, blood-bright spheres:
They should be pendent from the ear
Of some cool woman of Vermeer.

The sun's glass worry-beads,
Jujube of July to the blackbird's
Elderberry eye – how they bleed

The hectic rose of its fever!
I thought I would stand there forever
With the green light washing over

Me, idle-handed, while the ribbed globe
Of each berry ripened its glow.
I suppose what held me was that slow

Transfusion of all the senses, leaving
Me shadowless, opaque, suspended of belief.
Until, that is, the blackbird lifted

In its epicurean bill
This sacrament, a single ruby
To the sun's dark crucible.

Interregnum

This morning earth tilts to a new angle.
Dew so dense it is a liquid frost –
First fleece of winter
And the air quickens the ice crystal
In the robin's song.

It is the hour before doing:
Shadows stand ajar in their deep thirst
Waiting for time to enter.
There is no name for the hour that stalls
Like a plum between seasons

Where desire and fear mingle –
The tart and the dulcet engrossed
In one disintegration.
Summer hangs in the womb, a caul
Of autumn on her, ransomed.

I pick a plum, and down the single
Furrow of its making wrest
The two halves' sweetness, disinter
The pip, and taste this hour's chill,
Its ripeness, and its reason.

Fons et Origo
(for the three of us)

This is the first flung
Window wide after winter.
This is a half drawn breath.
This is the unquestioned answer
Between larksong and larksong –
Heaven in a handsbreadth.

This, this is a loving long
Look at the lineaments of death.
It is stalk, and cup, and acorn.

Airlift

She's playing aeroplanes,
Airlifting her child into
A sky so clear so blandly blue

Palm pressed to palm
Her feet against his chest
Lifting; he is a parachutist

Reversed, freefaller
Rising, limbs spreadeagled
In the void that's prodigal

Of headroom as the halls
Of death. Steady and hard
Against her soles his eightmonth heart

Beats, the ribcage supple
As any bird's, less frail
More vulnerable. Hearts fail

When death's a way of life.
Words fail. I close my grip
For the descent, the earth in eclipse.

Split Willow at Bathford

Alexis, that your birth –
The gash of it
In me – should constitute
A severance of age from youth
Is as approximate –
I know – a reckoning
As two half truths.

This hand pressed to this
Does not add up
To prayer (no more than lips
To lips make love), but division is
A need in us so deep –
Without we'd die in doubt
Of what death is.

There is a willow wholly
Split in two:
Through it your days flow.
Yet light has spliced it crown to bole –
As if by severance to show,
Sweet child, your proof in me
Of root and soul.

Airborne

Upupup! The light percussive
Of your lips, a chick's nib
Tapping in the shell – the womb!
The cell! your gaze like water
Questing at the window's sill;
Well, I will let it spill right over
Till it floods the whole window
And your face hangs luminous
As Betelgeuse in heaven. So
I would have the glass hold you for ever.

And as I lift, cropping your blonde
Head, the moon swings its sickle.
Silence. Then your low *mooaan*
Burdening the world – as if that blade
Had reaped the fullness of all pain.
Each day you grow further from home, blazing
Your trail through the tongue's galaxy,
And either my arms deceive me, or
The hour the dark tide cast you speechless
On my shore, you did weigh more.

Dark Vessel

A woman stands at the stairs' foot,
Her eyes closed, feeling the density
Of darkness steady her as a child cries out
In its sleep again, once, then silence.

Here are the couplings of time unhinged,
Her loose hands say. She is spooling back
To where the dormant frames lie lapped
And celibate as the fossil sleep of coiled things;

And it is a sort of language, flensed,
This listening, as into her heart's four
Chambers the cardinal winds pour
From the quartered rose. It is the fluency

Of one who sleepwalks into the poem
Which is the definitive history of memory.
Out of that ink-dark sea the cry
Of an oyster-catcher – once, again

Then silence. A lighthouse – Platte Fougère,
The Hanois – slides its wedge of sight
Through space, and she climbs into that light
And on and up the waves' salt stair

To where her children lie, nestled
At either hand, innocent of art
Or the origin of its costly freight – the port
And starboard lights of some dark vessel.

Cosmos and Mimosa

(for Alexis)

Da Capo

Just when you've spent your last obol
And the ferryman lays down his pole
For the long night, she disembarks from dream
Into broad day, like something out of a Chagall
And sexed and solid, a grounded angel
Picking her slow way back along the water's seam
With flowers for the living, her Thursday face
Half hidden behind the feathery greens
Moon discs and pollenbursts of Cosmos,
Of Mimosa. Follow her, for she has far to go.

Fundamental

In the first there was the vast
Black interior of the church.
I was fear and lust where the match
Sputtered, then caught, investing

Shadow with history's dark
Habit, the wick with its cowl
Of flame. Then there was that cool
Note, isolate as a spark

Struck from the quick of the flesh,
The soul's tuning fork –
Ut. That. – invoking
The whole gamut. Ashes

To ashes, you are other,
Unutterable other. Speechless
I knelt and wept for my loss,
For the woman that is your mother.

Mediant

Open
Close.
What struck the comma out?
Who fleshed the interval
Between the open fifth
Our voices made with this
This mediant, this and?

His
Hers.
Who dared democratise
The clause, the halt, the march
Of speech – broke wind, beat
Time, made apposite
The breath's subordinate?

First
Last.
Who struck the hour? What fire
Made twist, twist once, this strip
Of light to cinch the earth,
Splicing the ends of here
And there, inventing ever?

In
Out.
Doubt made the metaphor
And hope the möbius loop
And these made love made this.
Bisect. Our forgings lie
Apart – two noughts, one link.

Contrary Motion

Spreadeagled for sleep, godlike, on your back
In the long grass, after the close-hauled
Act, you lie willing the sky

To stand still. It's a confidence trick
You think (like faith, like sex, like all
Illusions of power) – when the key

Yields suddenly in the mind's lock
And the green raft slips its hausers,
Gliding back through the eye

Of unknowing. What lies in its wake,
In the ruffled skein of hours hauled
From the future, is a far cry.

The Water Carriers

It was a tunnel of rutted mud and thirst
Beneath the burden of mosquitoes,
The locked-out light screwing a fist
Where its prophecy was in our eyes.
Out of the mulch of sweetchestnut leaves
Came slugs with orange bellies.

We sang for air: our pitched breath
Sounding the vault for an afterlife,
And faltering at each echo's stillbirth.

Only the muffled percussive the jerricans
Made as they banged our shins
Troubled silence – as much as a skimmed
Stone grazes the water's skin.
It was a thousand years to the Chasseur's
Farm, two thousand back, the full cans
Wallowing, limbs straitjacketed by weight
Of water, our lungs bursting, mouths
Murderous with grenadine:

As out of a dream of drowning
The way we broke into the light
Was like a crowning.

Mimesis

Dragged, drenched, from sleep, by horror
Of smothering, I found your hot
Wet head too close to my heart.

Mortified by neglect following so hard
On your first breath, I cradled
Your head back to its own bed,

My fingers trembling while the swell
Of darkness stilled in the darker well
Of all wishing – your fontanelle;

Only to find you there, absolute and apart
In unrippled sleep, no more a part
Of me than this mockery of the art

Of mothering: my own breast taut
With a need in these hands so hot
It wept milk straight from my chilled heart.

Triptych

I

First frost. The cumulus of breath
We stoop through to collect the tart harvest;
Each day a different constellation, less
Random than the last. See how the grass
Retains the acid green and aftermath
Of weight, the precise gist of appleness.
Just so. The day your chilled fist
No longer fits in mine to take its warmth,
The apples and the frost will go unnoticed.

II

In this wide garden chance has planted
A child; hunkered in earth, neat as a bulb,
The nib of his head points heavenward.
He is all gathered in time, at the hub
Of the seasons' wheel, the only hour he knows –
The immutable noon of love when the big hand
And the little hand conjoin. Dusk loosens
Its damp knot. It is time to move on.
The heart quickens, then slows, to the thin
Bright beat of the bell at Evensong.

III

Daddy's boy. Not so. You are your own
Despite appearances; feet on the ground,
Running. In our belfry we wait for the wind
To come, speaking in broken whispers of
Ourselves, the rich dissonance of love.
When words fail, our breaths rise and fall
Across your name's hushed vocable.
What recalls us to ourselves is not the founding,
Nor the fundamental, but the low thrill
Of the hum note outliving the swung bell.

Perpetuum mobile

What made the mother
Of the boy with the corn-stalk hair
On a merry-go-round at the end of a pier
In a port on the edge of the map
Where the holiday stops
Stop and stare?

It wasn't the light
The late sun stitched up the water with,
Splinting the hulls and masts and their warped
Reflections, that jostled the rafts
Of the dark facades
Ceding to night.

Neither that, not this
Candescent coronet of glitz
With its lions and howdas and kids on waltzing
Skewbalds, spinning the world
On their axis, wild
With *it is, it is*.

Punctual as birthdays
They return the returning wave
Of the grownups down there with dazed faces
As the chattanooga choo-choo passes
And passes them by
Irrevocably.

Oh stop the calliope,
Call back the gaze of the child
With the darkening crop of hair from the vacancy
Where she stood, crying *Lente,*
Lente currite
Noctis equi.

Inverted Fugue

Out of the blue a child said: 'Yellow
Is God's colour.' How can a statement of fact
Be so open and so closed? It is the perfect
Cast of a child's mind, this allowing
Outward inwardness, and like the shell –
Whose whorls the precise vanishing-point of which
The amazed eye, triumphant, fails to detect –
Springs always backwards on the spiral
Of its own making. Perhaps it is the soul
Simply speaking itself, and like that act
Of faith, visionary as a lover's pact
With infinity, endlessly recalls
Creation. Alexis, this is your own doing,
The poem, the double helix of your being.

Envoi

Go, little bud of flame
Far from the hands' chalice
That dream themselves a calyx
For the quickening bloom

Of your face. Burn
With the wild white fire
Of your four years, far
From the pen's gravid burin,

The poem's epitaph.
Plant in their place the white
Flowers of Cosmos for the world
The word knows the beauty of;

And the February sunbursts
Of Mimosa for that art
For which the blind mimetic heart
Beats beneath this breast.

One day you'll ask what happens when you die
And I shall say a part of you steps out
Of time forever, and another so deeply in

It travels the centuries of thought that die
Are conceived and born and die again out
There where the wind gathers its harvest in

Among the stars that know what it is to die
Yet go on shining after their light's put out
On the hunched fear that let the darkness in